CORE LIBRARY OF US STATES

PUERTO RICO

BY RICHARD SEBRA

CONTENT CONSULTANT
Camilla Stevens, PhD
Professor, Department of Spanish and Portuguese
Rutgers University

Core Library

An Imprint of Abdo Publishing
abdobooks.com

abdobooks.com

Published by Abdo Publishing, a division of ABDO, PO Box 398166, Minneapolis, Minnesota 55439. Copyright © 2023 by Abdo Consulting Group, Inc. International copyrights reserved in all countries. No part of this book may be reproduced in any form without written permission from the publisher. Core Library™ is a trademark and logo of Abdo Publishing.

Printed in the United States of America, North Mankato, Minnesota.
052022
092022

THIS BOOK CONTAINS
RECYCLED MATERIALS

Cover Photo: Laura Graphenteen
Interior Photos: Maremagnum/Corbis Documentary/Getty Images, 4–5; Red Line Editorial, 9 (Puerto Rico), 9 (USA); Sarin Images/Granger, 10–11, 12; Shutterstock Images, 15 (flag), 15 (flower), 15 (tree); W. Marissen/iStockphoto, 15 (bird); Mark Margerison/iStockphoto, 15 (frog); Universal History Archive/Universal Images Group/Getty Images, 17, 43; Felix Lipov/Shutterstock Images, 22–23; Alisha Bube/iStockphoto, 26; Alessandro Pietri/Shutterstock Images, 28; Holly Mazour/Shutterstock Images, 30–31; Israel Pabon/Shutterstock Images, 34, 45; Richard Ellis/Alamy, 36–37; Photo File/MLB Photos/Getty Images Sport Classic/Getty Images, 39

Editor: Katharine Hale
Series Designer: Joshua Olson

Library of Congress Control Number: 2021951562

Publisher's Cataloging-in-Publication Data

Names: Sebra, Richard, author.
Title: Puerto Rico / by Richard Sebra
Description: Minneapolis, Minnesota : Abdo Publishing, 2023 | Series: Core library of US states | Includes online resources and index.
Identifiers: ISBN 9781532197802 (lib. bdg.) | ISBN 9781098270568 (ebook)
Subjects: LCSH: U.S. states--Juvenile literature. | Puerto Rico--Relations--United States--Juvenile literature. | Puerto Rico--History--Juvenile literature. | Physical geography--United States--Juvenile literature.
Classification: DDC 972.95--dc23

Population demographics broken down by race and ethnicity come from the 2019 census estimate. Population totals come from the 2020 census.

CONTENTS

ISLA DEL ENCANTO

The sun shines brightly as a parade makes its way down a crowded city street. The parade is filled with people wearing colorful costumes. Some are wearing masks with horns and large teeth. Bands march down the street playing music. It is part of the annual Carnival celebration. This is held in February or March in the city of Ponce, Puerto Rico. People from across the region visit Ponce for Carnival. It also draws in many tourists from outside of Puerto Rico.

Ponce is sometimes called *La Perla del Sur*, or "Pearl of the South."

Puerto Rico is known as the *Isla del Encanto* in Spanish. That means the "Island of Enchantment." People have been enchanted by Puerto Rico for centuries. It has beautiful beaches. It has lush rain forests. And it has foggy mountain peaks.

PERSPECTIVES

ROSARIO DAWSON

Actress Rosario Dawson was born in New York. But her grandmother was Puerto Rican, and Dawson spent a lot of time on the island growing up. She feels a special connection to the Island of Enchantment. "You definitely feel recharged when you go there," she said. "But there's some of it that comes back with you, that kind of maintains that level of peace that you feel ripple through your life even after you leave."

UNIQUE TERRITORY

Puerto Rico may be the Island of Enchantment. But the territory of Puerto Rico actually includes many islands. There are more than 140 pieces of land of various sizes in the territory. Puerto Rico is the name of the largest island. That is where the capital and largest city of San Juan is.

The only other islands with permanent populations are Vieques, Culebra, and Old San Juan.

Some of Puerto Rico's other large cities are near San Juan, including Bayamón, Carolina, and Guayanabo. Caguas is the largest city in central Puerto Rico. Ponce is the largest city on the south coast, while Mayagüez is the largest city on the east coast.

Puerto Rico is located in the Caribbean. Puerto Rico is surrounded by the Atlantic Ocean to the north and the Caribbean Sea to the south. Other island nations in the area include the Dominican

THE CARIBBEAN

The Caribbean is a collection of more than 7,000 islands in the Caribbean Sea. The sea is located south of the Gulf of Mexico. Some coastlines of mainland Mexico, Central America, and South America border the Caribbean Sea. These areas are also part of the Caribbean. There are 13 Caribbean countries. Countries throughout the region import and export goods to and from Puerto Rico. The Caribbean is an important part of Puerto Rico's economy and culture.

Republic to the west and the US Virgin Islands to the east.

Puerto Rico is a territory of the United States. But in many ways, it is like a whole other country. Puerto Rico has a unique culture all its own. This culture has been shaped by the numerous people who have called the island home. The form of Spanish that people speak includes words from the native Taíno people. They lived on the island when it was colonized by Spain, and their descendants live there still. Many people also speak English. Spanish and English are both official languages of Puerto Rico.

Modern Puerto Rico faces challenges. Deadly hurricanes have damaged the country in recent years. Citizens debate whether it should become a US state. Others believe it should be its own country. But Puerto Ricans maintain a strong pride in their homeland. And people come from all over the world to experience it.

MAP OF
PUERTO RICO

This map shows some of Puerto Rico's largest cities. What do you notice about the general location of each of these cities? Why do you think large cities developed there?

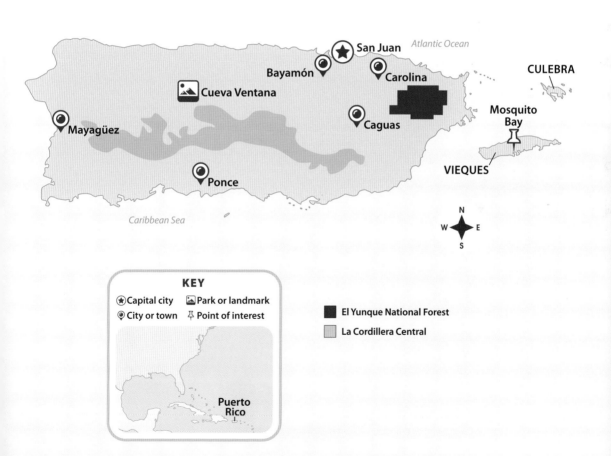

KEY

- ★ Capital city
- 📷 Park or landmark
- 📍 City or town
- ⚓ Point of interest

■ El Yunque National Forest
□ La Cordillera Central

HISTORY OF PUERTO RICO

People first came to Puerto Rico as early as 3000 BCE. The Taíno people later inhabited the island. The Taíno had originally come from Venezuela. They migrated to islands throughout the Caribbean. These people were well adapted to life on Puerto Rico. They made medicines from native plants. They used the island's materials to build canoes. The Taíno wrote poetry and music. And they played ball games. By 1000 CE, the Taíno were the dominant culture on the island.

Indigenous people were already living in the Caribbean when Europeans arrived.

Juan Ponce de León created the first European settlements in Puerto Rico.

EUROPEAN ARRIVAL

Christopher Columbus arrived in Puerto Rico in 1493. He was a European explorer. Columbus claimed the land for Spain. He did so even though the land was already occupied by thousands of Taíno people.

But it wasn't until 1508 that explorer Juan Ponce de León began to establish settlements on the island. He founded the town of Puerto Rico in 1521. *Puerto Rico* means "rich port" in Spanish. That later became the name of the entire island.

The Taíno welcomed the Spanish at first. But the Spanish soon enslaved the Taíno, forcing them into farming and mining work. Puerto Rico had many natural resources that Spain wanted.

Most of the Taíno died from disease. The germs that the Spanish carried were deadly to people who had never encountered them before. Within 50 years, almost all of the Taíno were gone. To replace them, the Spanish brought

PERSPECTIVES
RAMÓN EMETERIO BETANCES

Ramón Emeterio Betances was born in Puerto Rico in 1827. He went to medical school in Paris. He came back home to start a hospital in the middle of a cholera outbreak. Betances was also an activist. He fought to abolish slavery. The Spanish government had him removed from the country for it. Betances is best remembered for leading the Puerto Rico independence movement. In 1867 he published "Ten Commandments of Free Men." This document outlined what Puerto Ricans required to truly be free. Betances continued working for abolition while living in France, where he died in 1898.

enslaved Africans to the island. The Spanish forced these enslaved people to farm sugarcane and ginger. Slavery was the main source of labor in Puerto Rico until it was abolished in 1873.

Indigenous, European, and African populations intermarried over hundreds of years. This created the unique makeup of modern Puerto Rico. Many Puerto Ricans today consider themselves of Indigenous descent.

Spain tried to increase Puerto Rico's agricultural output to make the colony more profitable. More agricultural opportunities drew people to Puerto Rico. The population of the island increased from 45,000 in 1765 to 155,000 by 1800. People came from other Spanish colonies and other countries. Even more people, mostly from Spain, came throughout the 1800s. By 1890 the population had reached almost 1 million.

Puerto Rico began to develop its own culture in the late 1800s. People began to push for Puerto Rico to be

PUERTO RICO
QUICK FACTS

Study the information below. What do Puerto Rico's nickname and symbols tell you about the territory's landscape?

Abbreviation: PR
Nickname: *Isla del Encanto* (Island of Enchantment)
Motto: *Joannes est nomen eius* (John is his name)
Date of becoming a US territory: March 2, 1917
Capital: San Juan
Population: 3,285,874
Area: 5,325 square miles (13,792 sq km)

SYMBOLS

National symbol
Coquí frog

Official flower
Flor de Maga

Official bird
Puerto Rican spindalis

Official tree
Ceiba

its own country. But Spain wanted to keep control of its colony. It offered more rights to Puerto Ricans in 1897. It gave them all the rights of Spanish citizens and allowed Puerto Rico to have its own limited government.

US TERRITORY

Cuba is another island in the Caribbean. It was also a colony of Spain. Cuba began a war of independence in 1895. This affected US trade with Cuba. People in the United States were also concerned for Cuban citizens. These citizens were being treated poorly by the Spanish. The United States warned Spain it would intervene if hostilities did not stop. Then a US ship in the Cuban capital of Havana sank under mysterious circumstances. Responsibility was never proven, but the American people blamed the Spanish. The Spanish-American War (1898) began. The United States defeated the Spanish army in Cuba. US forces also

The Spanish-American War lasted less than a year. The war was largely fought at sea.

invaded Puerto Rico. They set up a military government there. The war ended in December of 1898.

The United States replaced the military government with a civilian one in 1900. Puerto Rico became a US territory in 1917. At that time, Puerto Ricans became US citizens. The United States set up a new government much like its own. There are three branches. The judicial branch includes the Supreme Court of Puerto Rico. This court interprets the territory's laws. The legislative

OTHER US TERRITORIES

The United States includes five self-governing territories. They are American Samoa, Guam, the Northern Mariana Islands, Puerto Rico, and the US Virgin Islands. Though these territories govern themselves, they fall under US authority. The United States has gained territories in different ways. For instance, the queen of Spain ceded Guam to the United States. The United States bought the Virgin Islands from Denmark. Territories sometimes become states. Alaska and Hawaii are states that were once US territories.

branch includes two houses of Congress. They are the Senate and the Chamber of Representatives. Congress makes the laws. The executive branch is led by the governor. The governor is the head of the Puerto Rican government. The chief of state for Puerto Rico is the US president. However, Puerto Rican citizens cannot vote for president. This is one of the reasons there is a debate over whether Puerto Rico should remain a US territory.

THE STATEHOOD DEBATE

In 1952 Puerto Rico became a commonwealth of the United States. That allowed it to have its own constitution. Commonwealth status was approved by a majority of voting Puerto Ricans. But many people were angry. They believed Puerto Rico should be its own country. Some people participated in violent protests.

Debates about Puerto Rico's future continue today. Some Puerto Ricans want it to remain a US territory. Others believe Puerto Rico should become a US state or its own country. These debates intensified in the late 2010s and early 2020s. Hurricane Maria did major damage to the island in 2017. The COVID-19 pandemic raged across the island in 2020. Many Puerto Ricans were unhappy with the US government's response to these disasters. Some people felt the US government would have a better response if Puerto Rico were a state. Others think the US government should not be involved at all. There are many points of view on this debate. In 2020 Puerto Ricans voted in favor of becoming a state. But not everyone voted, and it was a narrow majority. The US Congress has to approve statehood. These details may keep Congress from voting on Puerto Rican statehood. Experts expect the debate to continue.

STRAIGHT TO THE
SOURCE

Jenniffer González-Colón is Puerto Rico's representative in the US House of Representatives. But she does not get to vote. She believes this leaves the citizens she represents without a voice:

> *It is long past time for the federal government to put Puerto Rico on the path to equality. The Americans of this territory—including the 235,000 who have served in the Armed Forces—deserve equality. Territory status, with its lack of representation and lesser treatment than that of the States, has caused most Puerto Ricans to obtain the privileges of statehood by moving to a State. They earn more than twice as much as if they had remained here and have a poverty rate that is less than half.*

Source: Jenniffer González-Colón. "Statement from Congresswoman Jenniffer Gonzalez on Puerto Rico's Statehood Vote." *US Congresswoman Jenniffer González-Colón*, 10 Nov. 2020, gonzalez-colon.house.gov. Accessed 22 Apr. 2021.

BACK IT UP

The author of this passage is using evidence to support a point. Write a paragraph describing the point the author is making. Then write down two or three pieces of evidence the author uses to make the point.

GEOGRAPHY AND CLIMATE

Puerto Rico is well known as an island. But it actually is an archipelago. It consists of many islands. The main island of Puerto Rico is by far the biggest one.

Most of the interior of the main island is mountains. The main mountain range is *La Cordillera Central,* or "Central Range." The Central Range runs east to west. It divides the island into north and south. It contains the highest peak on the island. Cerro de Punta is 4,390 feet (1,338 m) tall.

Puerto Rico has mountains and forests as well as beaches.

23

PERSPECTIVES

MAGIC BEACHES

Puerto Rico has beautiful beaches any time of day. But at night, some beaches take on a totally different look. Mosquito Bay on the island of Vieques is often referred to as magical. Tiny life-forms in the water can light up when they bump against each other. This phenomenon is called bioluminescence. The light appears brightest when there is no moonlight. Many companies offer boat tours to experience the light up close. One visitor said, "Kayaking through the glowing waters of Mosquito Bay is one of the greatest experiences of my life. Each paddle stroke gave off a radiant blue shine. . . . A beautiful starry sky above, and bright lights below."

The northern and southern sides of Puerto Rico are coastal. They are lined with beaches. Puerto Rico has approximately 300 miles (480 km) of coastline. The coastal areas are where most people live. The Puerto Rico Trench north of the island is the deepest trench of the Atlantic Ocean. Its deepest point is 27,493 feet (8,380 m) below the surface.

Puerto Rico has no natural lakes. But it

has some small rivers. Most of them come out of the Central Range.

TROPICAL PARADISE

Like all Caribbean islands, Puerto Rico has a tropical climate. It is hot and humid most of the year. Puerto Rico has only two seasons. It has a wet season that lasts from April to November. More than 80 percent of the yearly rain falls in these months. Dry season lasts from December to March. These months are slightly cooler.

It does not get very cold in Puerto Rico. The lowest temperature on record was 40 degrees Fahrenheit (4°C). The highest temperature was 104 degrees Fahrenheit (40°C).

As an island, Puerto Rico has many plants and animals only found there. A lot of them live in El Yunque National Forest. This is the only tropical rain forest in the US Forest System.

Puerto Rico has no native land mammals. The only mammals native to Puerto Rico are 13 types of bats.

Visitors to El Yunque can see waterfalls, tropical plants and animals, and more.

But it has many native species of reptiles and amphibians. The coquí frog is named for the "co-kee" sound it makes. Many people consider the coquí frog a symbol of Puerto Rico. Like the frog, Puerto Rico is small and resilient with a big voice.

Birds found only in Puerto Rico include the Puerto Rican screech owl and Puerto Rican spindalis. There used to be approximately 1 million Puerto Rican parrots on the island. But deforestation has reduced the population to only a few dozen. Researchers are making efforts to restore the parrot population.

NATURAL DISASTERS

Climate change poses several threats for Puerto Rico. The island has long been in danger of hurricanes. Warming ocean temperatures have increased the intensity and number of storms. Scientists estimate a major storm like Hurricane Maria

THE CEIBA TREE

The ceiba tree has been important to Puerto Ricans for centuries. The Taíno people used it to make canoes. Puerto Ricans love to gather around the winding trunks of ceiba trees still today. One famous tree on the island of Vieques has stood for hundreds of years. It was alive during Spanish rule. It survived bombing practice from the US Navy. And it survived Hurricane Maria. It lost all its leaves and flowers and some branches after the hurricane. Two years later, it started to bloom again. The tree is a national symbol of Puerto Rico. It reminds Puerto Ricans that they can always come back from disaster.

Hurricane Maria caused widespread damage in Puerto Rico.

was five times more likely to occur in the 2010s than in the 1950s.

Hurricane Maria killed 3,000 people and did billions of dollars in damage in 2017. People were left without power and basic services for months. The hurricane destroyed habitat for animals and caused severe flooding.

The island was still recovering from Maria when Hurricane Dorian hit in 2019. Dorian was a much weaker hurricane. But frequent hurricanes leave Puerto Rico with less time to recover from previous storms.

Rising temperatures lead to rising sea levels. Puerto Rico's ocean waters have risen 4 inches (10 cm) since 1960. They could rise as much as 3 feet (0.9 m) in the next 100 years. That would flood coastal areas. It would put needed farmland underwater.

FURTHER EVIDENCE

Chapter Three covers some of the geographic areas of Puerto Rico. What was one of the main points of this chapter? What evidence is included to support this point? Read the article at the website below. Does the information on the website support the main point of the chapter? Does it present new evidence?

ABOUT EL YUNQUE NATIONAL FOREST

abdocorelibrary.com/puerto-rico

RESOURCES AND ECONOMY

Since Spain began colonizing Puerto Rico, farming has been an important industry on the island. The Spanish enslaved the Taíno people to farm sugarcane, tobacco, coffee, and more. They later brought in enslaved people from Africa to work in the fields.

Modern Puerto Ricans do not do much farming. There is not enough agricultural output to support the population. Puerto Rico imports 85 percent of its food supply.

Coffee is one of the main agricultural products of Puerto Rico.

PERSPECTIVES

DR. CABRERA

Eileen Diaz Cabrera is a doctor in Puerto Rico. Her practice was tested during Hurricane Maria. With the island mostly out of power, Cabrera's office had to run off a generator. And there was only so much fuel for it. Her work in tough conditions helped save lives. "We opened because we knew the patients needed us," she said. "We knew there were emergencies we could treat in the office and that there would be patients without prescriptions or those whose insulin had been damaged by the lack of refrigeration."

But sugarcane and coffee are still farmed on the island. Other crops include pineapples and bananas.

FACTORIES AND MEDICINE

US companies started to build factories in Puerto Rico in the 1940s. Manufacturing has been the biggest industry there ever since. One industry stands out among all the manufacturing. Puerto Rico is one of the world's leading manufacturers of medicine. Eleven of the top 20 drug companies in the world have factories in Puerto Rico. These companies manufacture various medicines.

More than half of the world's best-selling medicines are made there. Puerto Rico exported $13.1 billion of medicine in 2020. It is by far the island's most valuable export.

TOURISM

With its beaches and warm weather, Puerto Rico is also a top tourist destination. Millions of people visit every year. Puerto Rico is also a popular destination for cruise ships.

Puerto Rico is very easy for US citizens to visit. Since it is a US territory, visitors do not need passports.

MIGRATION

People leaving the island is one economic challenge for Puerto Rico. They leave the island for other opportunities. There are more Puerto Ricans living on the US mainland than on the island. Lots of people began migrating to the mainland in the 1950s. The shift from farming to manufacturing caused many people to leave the island for work. Factors such as Hurricane Maria accelerated the rate of people leaving. The population decreased by 142,000 people from 2017 to 2018. One-third of those people moved to Florida. Florida has a large Puerto Rican population. New York is another major destination.

They can also spend US money. And many people in Puerto Rico speak English.

Puerto Rico has a poverty rate higher than any US state. But poverty has been declining in recent years. And there is a growing middle class. Puerto Rico still faces economic challenges. In 2021 it was still recovering from Hurricane Maria. The government has had to borrow a lot of money. These problems have led to people leaving the island for the United States. This loss of workers has hurt the economy even more.

EXPLORE ONLINE

Chapter Four talks about the effects of hurricanes on Puerto Rico's economy. The article at the website below goes into more detail about hurricanes. Does this article answer any questions you have about Puerto Rico's hurricanes?

HURRICANE
abdocorelibrary.com/puerto-rico

Puerto Rico's beaches and wildlife make it a popular tourist destination.

PEOPLE AND PLACES

Puerto Ricans take a lot of pride in their heritage and identity. Their identity has been shaped by all the different people from Puerto Rico's past. That includes European and American colonists. It includes Indigenous people and enslaved Africans. Many identify themselves as Puerto Rican, not American, regardless of whether they were born in Puerto Rico or on the US mainland. Some call themselves Boricua. This comes from Borikén, the Taíno word for the island.

Bomba is a traditional Puerto Rican dance originally created by enslaved Africans brought to the island.

Many Puerto Ricans living on the US mainland maintain close connections to the island.

PERSPECTIVES

ROBERTO CLEMENTE

Roberto Clemente was one of the first big baseball stars from Puerto Rico. He saw himself as a representative of all Latin America, not just Puerto Rico. "Always, they said Babe Ruth was the best there was," he said. "They said you'd really have to be something to be like Babe Ruth. But Babe Ruth was an American player. What we needed was a Puerto Rican player they could say that about, someone to look up to and try to equal." Clemente was also known for his charity work. He was killed in a plane crash while on his way to help victims of an earthquake in Nicaragua in 1972.

MUSIC AND SPORTS

A big part of Puerto Rican culture is music. Puerto Ricans enjoy many kinds of music. These include salsa, bomba, and jazz. Puerto Rico has produced many famous musicians such as Tito Puente and Ricky Martin.

Many Puerto Ricans enjoy sports. Baseball is a national obsession. There have

Roberto Clemente was a Puerto Rican baseball player. He played 18 seasons with the Pittsburgh Pirates.

been many big leaguers and several Hall of Famers from Puerto Rico. Puerto Rican players include All-Stars Yadier Molina and José Berrios. Puerto Rico competes as its own country in many international baseball competitions.

PLACES TO GO

There are many unique places to visit in Puerto Rico. People enjoy hiking in the El Yunque National Forest

PUERTO RICAN CUISINE

Much like Puerto Rican people, Puerto Rican food is a blend of different cultures. It is influenced by Spanish, African, American, and Taíno cuisines. One of Puerto Rico's national dishes is *arroz con gandules*. That means "rice with pigeon peas." This dish contains rice, a type of peas called pigeon peas, and smoked ham. Many popular dishes in Puerto Rico are based around rice. Puerto Rico is also surrounded by all sorts of fresh seafood.

or kayaking on scenic bays. Another landmark is *Cueva Ventana* or "window cave" near Arecibo. It is Puerto Rico's only natural cave and is one of its most popular tourist attractions. History lovers flock to Old San Juan. This historic district includes old Spanish fortresses such as Castillo San Felipe del Morro.

There are many things Puerto Ricans love about their home. The island is as varied as the people who live there. They remain enchanted by it still today.

STRAIGHT TO THE
SOURCE

Journalism student Kailey Latham interviewed Puerto Rican students, asking about their national identity. Gabriela Joglar Burrowes is a student at the University of Puerto Rico. She said:

> *I feel that I'm Puerto Rican, and I think I'm Puerto Rican because I think my culture is different from that from, say, somewhere in the United States. Puerto Ricans, we're defined by our history, by our namesake; we have our own groups, we have our own food, we have our own [way] of being.*

Source: Kailey Latham. "Statehood Issue Stirs Passions about Puerto Rican Identity." *Puerto Rico: Unsettled Territory*, 29 Oct. 2012, cronkite.asu.edu. Accessed 6 June 2021.

WHAT'S THE BIG IDEA?

Take a close look at this passage. How does Burrowes view her national identity? How do the geography and culture of Puerto Rico contribute to her point of view?

IMPORTANT DATES

1000

The Taíno culture is the dominant culture on the island they call Borikén.

1493

A Spanish expedition led by Christopher Columbus becomes the first European presence on the island.

1508

Juan Ponce de León begins establishing settlements on the island.

1521

The town of Puerto Rico is established, which eventually becomes the name for the entire island.

1898

US forces invade Puerto Rico during the Spanish-American war. The war ends in December with Spain's defeat.

1917

Puerto Rico becomes a US territory.

1952

Puerto Rico approves its first constitution.

2017

Hurricane Maria devastates the island, killing thousands of people and causing billions of dollars in damage.

STOP AND
THINK

Tell the Tale

Chapter One of this book describes the Carnival celebration in Ponce. Imagine you are attending this celebration. Write 200 words about the things you see and hear. What do you enjoy most about the celebration?

Surprise Me

Chapter Two discusses Puerto Rico's history. After reading this book, what two or three facts about Puerto Rico's history did you find most surprising? Write a few sentences about each fact. Why did you find each fact surprising?

Dig Deeper

After reading this book, what questions do you still have about Puerto Rico? With an adult's help, find a few reliable sources that can help you answer your questions. Write a paragraph about what you learned.

Another View

This book discusses Puerto Rico's status as a US territory. As you know, every source is different. Ask a librarian or another adult to help you find another source about this topic. Write a short essay comparing and contrasting the new source's point of view with that of this book's author. What is the point of view of each author? How are they similar and why? How are they different and why?

GLOSSARY

cede
to give up land or
power to another

cholera
an intestinal disease
usually caused by drinking
contaminated water

colony
an area of land that is
separate from but controlled
by another country

deforestation
clearing trees from an area

economy
a place's system of goods,
services, money, and jobs

habitat
the place where a plant or an
animal lives

Indigenous
relating to the earliest known
residents of an area

mammal
a type of animal with
certain characteristics such
as producing milk and
having fur

poverty
having very little money
or resources

rain forest
an area with lots of trees
and wet, rainy conditions for
much of the year

ONLINE RESOURCES

To learn more about Puerto Rico, visit our free resource websites below.

Visit **abdocorelibrary.com** or scan this QR code for free Common Core resources for teachers and students, including vetted activities, multimedia, and booklinks, for deeper subject comprehension.

Visit **abdobooklinks.com** or scan this QR code for free additional online weblinks for further learning. These links are routinely monitored and updated to provide the most current information available.

LEARN MORE

Kramer, Barbara. *Lin-Manuel Miranda.* Abdo, 2018.

Sillett, Julia. *Hurricanes Harvey, Irma, Maria, and Nate.* Crabtree, 2019.

INDEX

About the Author

Richard Sebra is a children's book author and journalist. He and his wife enjoy cooking, surfing, and hiking with their dogs.